Elf~help for Raising a Teen

Elf~help for Raising a Teen

written by
Jim Auer

illustrated by
R.W. Alley

ONE CARING PLACE

Abbey Press

Text © 2000 by Jim Auer
Illustrations © 2000 by St. Meinrad Archabbey
Published by One Caring Place
Abbey Press
St. Meinrad, Indiana 47577

Library of Congress Catalog Number
00-100729

ISBN 0-87029-336-2

Printed in the United States of America

Foreword

You knew it, of course, the day your child was born—even if you didn't consciously think of it at the time: Thirteen years later this child would become...a *teenager*. The very word evokes mixed feelings: excitement, pride, concern, conflict—maybe even danger.

The journey through the teen years must be undertaken by both teen and parent. It's exceptionally energy-consuming and emotionally draining for both parties. And no two journeys are exactly alike, for either teen or parent, even within the same family. Each parent-teen relationship has its unique highs and lows, strains and rewards.

In the daily busyness of raising children, keeping a household, and making a living, it can be hard to pull together the skills and strategies you need to raise a teen. This mini manual can point the way. A handy collection of essential guidelines, it includes concrete suggestions for enriching, healing, and enjoying your relationship with your teen.

May this little volume help you to navigate your teen's teens with patience and love.

1.

Life hands us many jobs
and roles. Being the parent
of a teen is one of the most
demanding and important.
Feel genuinely important—
but not intimidated. Believe
in yourself.

2.

Parenting a teen is not like staging a space launch: if you program in the right information and push the right buttons, your child's journey to adulthood will be smooth and flaw-free. Expect glitches— and realize that they can bring growth on both sides.

3.

Remember your own adolescence as vividly as possible. Recall specific things you worried about, agonized over, were confused by, and rejoiced in. Compare them with your teen's concerns. You may find he is not such a stranger!

4.

Share some of the things that worried, confused, and delighted you as a teenager. Many things really are "different these days," but others remain the same. This sharing can tear down walls and keep <u>you</u> from seeming like a stranger.

5.

"You just don't understand!" is a catchphrase of the teen years. Expect to hear it. Realize that sometimes it might be <u>true</u>! Instead of trying to prove the statement wrong, say, "Maybe I don't, but I'd like to. Help me to understand."

6.

If your teen seems to become two or three different persons in the course of a day, this is normal. After all, it occasionally happens to adults, too. No one's temperament is an unvarying constant. What matters is responding to the "teen of the moment" with love.

7.

Teens often feel things more intensely than seems logical or sensible to adults. Accept this. Helping your teen to understand and cope is far better than telling him, "There's just no reason" to feel so strongly. "I'm sorry you're hurting" is a much better response than "It's not the end of the world."

8.

Keep a sense of humor,
especially in trying times.
Finding something to laugh
about does not belittle or
minimize a serious situation.
Laughter is often the spark that
helps people become more
willing to resolve the situation.

9.

Teens often feel that "right now is forever," especially when life seems troubled. Be careful not to absorb this outlook yourself. Gently try to help your teen realize that this is virtually never true.

N.B

10.

Some things really will matter tomorrow and a year from now; others won't. Teach your teen how to make this important distinction, using examples from your own life.

11.

A hug or pat on the shoulder is often worth a thousand words. If your teen resists, don't force it, but don't give up either. Await the next opportunity. An honest "I could really use a hug" often can melt the awkwardness.

12.

Recall happy times you have had with your child. Look at photos in your family album, and share them with your teen at an appropriate time. Visual reminders of bonding can create further bonding.

13.

Delightful surprises strengthen any relationship, especially for "no reason except that I love you." Arrange a delightful surprise for your teen every now and then.

14.

Check the proportion of positives and negatives in the messages you give your teen. Unless he is consistently sabotaging his life, send a much higher proportion of positive messages.

15.

Written messages are sometimes easier and better—whether they express praise, love, advice, or warning. Carefully worded notes can avert "But I thought you said…." Notes of praise and love can be kept and reread at low moments when a teen needs reassurance.

16.

A delicate conversation sometimes happens better in a car (especially to or from an ice-cream outing), rather than eyeball-to-eyeball. Take a circuitous route and order extra toppings!

17.

Communication—questions, suggestions, or requests—will often fail when we approach a teen at a bad time. If this happens frequently, discuss one another's best times to talk, okay times, and times to be avoided except for genuine emergencies.

18.

Some "heavy" conversations with teens need to take place almost immediately. Others are better left for a more appropriate time. When such conversations are needed, ask God for the wisdom to know the right time and approach.

19.

The tone of voice you use to say, "We need to have a talk," can make all the difference in whether the talk really happens—and is productive—or not.

20.

"Love can hurt" is literally a fact of human existence. This is especially true when you have to discipline a teen and withstand her responding animosity. It helps to remind yourself that, in trying to keep your teen on the right path, you are genuinely loving her.

21.

Avoid saying, "You always…" or "You never…," which are toxic accusations that cloud the actual issue. If you hear them from your teen, say, "I don't think that's either fair or true—and it hurts to hear you say that."

22.

"I love you," "I am disappointed
in what you've done," and
"I am proud of you for many
things" are not conflicting
messages. They can be said
all on the same occasion.
And usually should be.

23.

People make mistakes, and parents of teens are no exception. Forgive yourself— you're not a failure as a parent. Apologize to your teen, if needed. This does not undermine your authority; rather, it shows respect for your teen and models how to make amends for one's mistakes.

24.

It's unrealistic to expect a teen to acquire—simply from the distilled bits of wisdom you have offered him—the same perspective on life that you have acquired after several decades of living. Don't give up on imparting your experience; wait patiently for the seeds of wisdom to bear fruit.

25.

It's easy to focus on disagreements. List items you and your teen agree on— as weighty as the existence of God and as trivial as a favorite type of fast food. Keep this list and occasionally add to it.

26.

Seeking counseling is not a sign of instability or incompetence as a teen's parent. It simply acknowledges that you are not all-knowing. Wise people know they can profit from others' insights.

27.

Take some time to recall the things you've obviously done <u>right</u> as a parent. Remember that none of them are lost, no matter how things appear or feel at the moment.

28.

Parents need to encourage a teen's effort and growth. But comparing her unfavorably to someone else is damaging. Accept your teen for the unique (though not fully formed) young person she is.

29.

You have a right to expect
your teen to become a good
and honorable young person.
Unflinchingly insist on this.
It is not realistic, however, to
expect her to become a facsimile
of you. Do not insist on that.

30.

It's tempting for a teen to think, "It's _my_ life." Teach your teen that life is like a speedboat: we are responsible for the waves we make that impact others' lives. We do not live alone on a private lake.

31.

Strangely, it's easy to think, "This is war!" about relatively small things (like hairstyle) and, "Oh, well, it's a stage," about genuinely serious things (like a beginning pattern of drinking). Pray for the wisdom to tell the difference.

32.

Being nosy about a teen's friends and activities may be the "ultimate sin" from a teen's point of view, but it's also a parental duty. When you feel real uneasiness about a serious issue, be positively nosy. Many a teen later wishes his parents had been.

33.

It's painful when a teen challenges or seems to abandon the faith in which you raised her. Recall again that "now is not forever." Speak your disappointment candidly but gently, and turn the rest over to God.

34.

Learn from others. Parents who later think, "I wish I had spent more time with my teen," probably outnumber 1000-1 those who think, "I wish I had spent more time refinishing the dining room woodwork."

35.

If you temporarily have to spend a disproportionate amount of time on your job or some other task, talk this over with your family. Let your teen know that she is still your priority and you will change the situation as soon as you can.

36.

Study after study reports that, by most teens' own testimony, parents are the single most important influence in their lives. Believe this—especially when it doesn't seem believable.

37.

Studies also show that, according to teens, parents rank at the top of their list of heroes. Believe this and bask in a bit of justified glow.

ELF HOLLOW GOOD DEEDS AWARDS

38.

It's often said that God doesn't give us more than we can handle. But this is not a guarantee of smooth and sure passage through your child's teens. Hold on tightly to a belief in your own strength, and trust that God will provide the wisdom you need. Then enjoy the adventure!

Jim Auer has taught teenagers for over thirty years. He is the author of eleven books and over 300 articles, most of them for teens and young adults. He and his wife have been married for thirty years and are the parents of two former teenagers.

Illustrator for the Abbey Press Elf-help Books, **R.W. Alley** also illustrates and writes children's books. He lives in Barrington, Rhode Island, with his wife, daughter, and son.

The Story of the Abbey Press Elves

The engaging figures that populate the Abbey Press "elf-help" line of publications and products first appeared in 1987 on the pages of a small self-help book called *Be-good-to-yourself Therapy*. Shaped by the publishing staff's vision and defined in R.W. Alley's inventive illustrations, they lived out author Cherry Hartman's gentle, self-nurturing advice with charm, poignancy, and humor.

Reader response was so enthusiastic that more Elf-help Books were soon under way, a still-growing series that has inspired a line of related gift products.

The especially endearing character featured in the early books—sporting a cap with a mood-changing candle in its peak—has since been joined by a spirited female elf with flowers in her hair.

These two exuberant, sensitive, resourceful, kindhearted, lovable sprites, along with their lively elfin community, reveal what's truly important as they offer messages of joy and wonder, playfulness and co-creation, wholeness and serenity, the miracle of life and the mystery of God's love.

With wisdom and whimsy, these little creatures with long noses demonstrate the elf-help way to a rich and fulfilling life.

Elf-help Books

Elf-help for Raising a Teen
#20102 $4.95   ISBN 0-87029-336-2

Elf-help for Being a Good Parent
#20103 $4.95   ISBN 0-87029-335-4

Gratitude Therapy
#20105 $4.95   ISBN 0-87029-332-X

Garden Therapy
#20116 $4.95   ISBN 0-87029-325-7

Elf-help for Busy Moms
#20117 $4.95   ISBN 0-87029-324-9

Trust-in-God Therapy
#20119 $4.95   ISBN 0-87029-322-2

Elf-help for Overcoming Depression
#20134 $4.95   ISBN 0-87029-315-X

New Baby Therapy
#20140 $4.95   ISBN 0-87029-307-9

Grief Therapy for Men
#20141 $4.95   ISBN 0-87029-306-0

Living From Your Soul
#20146 $4.95   ISBN 0-87029-303-6

Teacher Therapy
#20145 $4.95   ISBN 0-87029-302-8

Be-good-to-your-family Therapy
#20154 $4.95   ISBN 0-87029-300-1

Stress Therapy
#20153 $4.95   ISBN 0-87029-301-X

Making-sense-out-of-suffering Therapy
#20156 $4.95   ISBN 0-87029-296-X

Get Well Therapy
#20157 $4.95   ISBN 0-87029-297-8

Anger Therapy
#20127 $4.95   ISBN 0-87029-292-7

Caregiver Therapy
#20164 $4.95   ISBN 0-87029-285-4

Self-esteem Therapy
#20165 $4.95   ISBN 0-87029-280-3

Take-charge-of-your-life Therapy
#20168 $4.95   ISBN 0-87029-271-4

Work Therapy
#20166 $4.95   ISBN 0-87029-276-5

Everyday-courage Therapy
#20167 $4.95   ISBN 0-87029-274-9

Peace Therapy
#20176 $4.95   ISBN 0-87029-273-0

Friendship Therapy
#20174 $4.95   ISBN 0-87029-270-6

Christmas Therapy (color edition)
#20175 $5.95   ISBN 0-87029-268-4

Grief Therapy
#20178 $4.95   ISBN 0-87029-267-6

Happy Birthday Therapy
#20181 $4.95   ISBN 0-87029-260-9

Forgiveness Therapy
#20184 $4.95   ISBN 0-87029-258-7

Keep-life-simple Therapy
#20185 $4.95   ISBN 0-87029-257-9

Celebrate-your-womanhood Therapy
#20189 $4.95   ISBN 0-87029-254-4

Acceptance Therapy (color edition)
#20182 $5.95   ISBN 0-87029-259-5

Acceptance Therapy
#20190 $4.95   ISBN 0-87029-245-5

Keeping-up-your-spirits Therapy
#20195 $4.95   ISBN 0-87029-242-0

Play Therapy
#20200 $4.95   ISBN 0-87029-233-1

Slow-down Therapy
#20203 $4.95   ISBN 0-87029-229-3

One-day-at-a-time Therapy
#20204 $4.95   ISBN 0-87029-228-5

Prayer Therapy
#20206 $4.95   ISBN 0-87029-225-0

Be-good-to-your-marriage Therapy
#20205 $4.95   ISBN 0-87029-224-2

Be-good-to-yourself Therapy (hardcover)
#20196 $10.95   ISBN 0-87029-243-9

Be-good-to-yourself Therapy
#20255 $4.95   ISBN 0-87029-209-9

Available at your favorite giftshop or bookstore—
or directly from One Caring Place, Abbey Press
Publications, St. Meinrad, IN 47577.
Or call 1-800-325-2511.